Heritage & Other Pseudonyms

Heritage & Other Pseudonyms

Lorrie Ness

Heritage & Other Pseudonyms
Copyright © 2024 Lorrie Ness

First Flowstone Press Edition • March 2024
ISBN 978-1-945824-65-4

Flowstone Press,
an Imprint of Left Fork

www.leftforkbooks.com

Portrait

Conception	3
Returning to Water	4
Stay-at-Home-Mom	5
Safety	6
Quarry	7
Crybaby Bridge	9
Rust Belt	11
Coming of Age	12
Janie's Elegy	14
Glitches	15
It Was Everyone. It Was No One.	16
Missing Pages	17
Collected Evidence	18
Daughter	20
By Choice	21
Body Language	22
Drapes	23
Body Cartography	24
Passing Zone	25
Deadfall	26
Facing Myself	27
I Ask Forgiveness	29
Reflections	31
Grace	32
Boundaries	33
Heavy Metal	34
Taxidermy	36
Muscle Memory	37
Refuge	38

Acrylic Garden	39
Cherry Pie	40
Anointing	41
Thresholds	42
Tic-Tac-Toe	44
Inheritance	45
What We Save	46
Mother's Letter	47
Haunted	48
Atonement	49
To My Brother Who Hardened	51
Say My Name	53
Blame	54
Ritual	55
Tire Swing	56
Cut Me a Switch	57
Whitewashed / Washedwhite	58
Because	59
Dreaming of Time	60
How Time Runs Out	61
Distillations	62
The Orange	64
Waiting for His Body	66
A Loyal Dog	68
Since October 2020	69
Taking the Dolls Home	70

Landscape

Diaspora	75
The Final Trip Home	76
Outside the Window	77
(g)round bones	79
That I May Feel Alive	80
Bottomland Bridges	81
Snapshot	82
Farm as a Silhouette	83
Better with Time	84
Carrying On	85
No Getting Away	86
Harvest	88
At the Table	89
Night Vision	90
Catching Crawdads	92
Milk Teeth	93
Plum	95
Charcoal on Water	96
Homecoming	97
Pond Water	98
Fight, Flight & Freeze	99
Compassion Fatigue	100
On Meeting a Shrike	102
Felling the Sycamore	103
Percolation	104
Acknowledgments	106
About the Author	108

Portrait

Conception

I was inside of her even then. As a point
of rupture, a follicle splitting apart her walls.
This was the beginning

of her hurt. The first time
he rutted against her skirt, in the parking lot,
tin cans still dangling from the bumper.

In a photograph
from the airport, she French braided her fingers
across her belly, tied the coat's belt

as a tourniquet — as if she felt my body puncture
and applied pressure to the tear.
This was the moment I began

dividing myself. One perimeter opening to another
is a body defined by entry. She learned
to shut out the world

later that year. Holding a baby.
Sitting for a photograph, knee atop knee, one foot
locked behind her heel,

as if wrapping flesh
around flesh could seal a wound. My lips, suckling.
Her mouth closed — barely even an arc.

Returning to Water

My finger glides along the rim,
circles the twilight

between our bodies.
Every birth leaves this depression.

A navel is the shape of loss. They tell me
she thumbed

the knotted cord like rosary, recited
the Apostles' Creed.

She believes in God, the father almighty,
creator of heaven and earth.

I take my first breath,
and lose everything I've ever known.

I find my way back by mapping the flesh —
putting a needle to the skin,

drawing each boundary as it's crossed.
Every line is my fault,

so I search your body
for the sea, for the safety of water

rushing my mouth.

Stay-at-Home-Mom

Purple plum, purple plum
   two kneecaps peeled from linoleum.

Mother was a nursery rhyme
who knew where to find the quarters that rolled away,

if my high bounce ball was wedged
beneath the fridge.

I played jacks by the oven,
where her mascara was smeared on the floor.

Quiet cause dad is sleeping.
She puckers,

cherry red, cherry red
takes two draws, sucks relentlessly

at the filter end.

Safety

A hundred yards north,
the first row of the corn field
is where home begins and ends.   Head east,
toes west, I lie in the space between
the stalks.   A hundred yards south
slapping & banging —
the summer song of our screen door,
where entrance & exit meet.   I push
leaves apart.

Blue sky browns
my skin.   A hundred yards north of the springs
croaking & dry wood backhanding
the jamb,   one uncle is coming inside,
a cousin is going out.
My shoulders are still
hugged in the furrow.   Above me, the ears
are silk-tasseled.

Their strands
rasp in the wind.   Louder than the constant pounding
of the door.

Quarry

I was 12 years old the first time
a strange man squinted his eyes at me, rocked back on his heels.

He wore overalls and when he puckered his lips, his whistle
groped my whole body. He'd been hunting

with my uncle, who'd walked the distance to the shed
with two limp rabbits swinging at his side.

My uncle left him there in the gravel drive to unkennel the dogs.
Us kids were piling into a truck as he leered.

I froze, with one foot on the top of the tire,
my other leg straddling the side panel of the pickup's bed.

Janie pulled me up and over the wheel well,
before his reaching hand could pat my rear. He brought his palm down

on the truck's red metal, gave it two good thumps instead —
but it was still my cheeks that burned.

So yous all cousins huh? Betchu boys like the looks of this one huh?
Now I don't wanna see no hanky panky.

He wagged his finger at us.
None of us spoke. I huddled close to Janie, the only other girl.

It never occurred to me that some people would fool around
with family members. It never occurred to me

that I'd be mistaken for the type who would.
Janie and I sat shoulder to shoulder looking down,

our uncombed mops hanging in front of our eyes.
It's not so much that our greasy hair had separated into clumps,

it's that the dirty strands clung together, as if bonded by the oil.
My oldest cousin put the truck in gear,

drove us over the washboard ruts bisecting field after yellow field.
In the pickup bed, our bodies swayed side to side in unison.

Crybaby Bridge

A coyote's forlorn howl pierced the air.
There was no sign of movement — a reminder that some dangers

could make themselves known, but never be seen.
We sought safety on the porch

& sat on milk pails filled with moonlight.
Our hair would wait for sunrise to burn off the dew.

Too hot to go back inside & too young to fall asleep.
We swapped legends about the haunting,

& worked up the courage to grab grandma's keys,
popsicles and a mixtape.

Headlights swept rows of corn & caught the eyes of deer.
It was after midnight

on Crybaby Bridge. We parked
in the ditch, waded through weeds to the water's edge.

Shhh... We listened for wailing,
waited for the woman in a glowing veil to surface

from below the ripples. That night, Janie was the only one
to walk into the creek. From shore

I watched her shadow drifting
downstream. A ghost —

save for the way her body blocked the stars
as she moved between the trestles

& disappeared.

Rust Belt

Everywhere, gravel cushions the fallen —
lipstick prints on filter ends, pull-tabs, and cellophane

from stores where even disposable things are still swaddled
in wrappers. Peeling from the billboard,

the single bright veneer still clinging to this street is stripping
slowly as the asphalt shingle siding

that transforms each of Janie's walls into ceiling. In a home built
from upper limits, only rainwater runs away

from this block. We launch paper boats along the curb,
grind shipwrecks underfoot. She and I, always

giggling as leaky pipes rot the studs,
as a little more Tyvek is lost to storms. Each plywood patch job

reclaims a shaft of light from the roof. It keeps hope alive,
squatting in an abandoned lot

to play a children's game. We tell fortunes
by tossing a ping pong ball on that gravel of fallen things.

Every throw finds its fate. Every bounce tells a chapter of the story.
She throws. I wait to see what it hits.

Glinting in the granite are beer bottles, condoms —
two eggshells in a cup of grass.

Coming of Age

Outside the 7-Eleven,
fluorescents flicker above the entrance.
Their color sallows the walls. Under the awning
only her shoulder blades, the sole of one flip flop,
touch the glass where she leans.

Janie is threadbare.

The gaps between her crossed arms & her body
do nothing to hide the soda cans glowing in the window,
hot dogs rolling under a heat lamp.

On the other side
of the glass. Customers scuttle, load their arms quickly.
They trade twenties for lotto tickets, pork rinds
and twelve packs of beer.

No one lingers.

Mosquitos halo the neon sign.
The electric hum of the lights may have dimmed their buzz
but this doesn't apply to her head — sagging

as a woman exits,
lights up a cigarette. She tilts her face and exhales,
scattering the cloud of bugs circling above. In that moment
only night air defines the distance
between them.

She doesn't speak.

Doesn't reach for the cash inside her pocket,
just holds out a pack of Newports, one tapped loose as an offering.
She understands

standing with someone is the cheapest form
of solidarity.

Janie's Elegy

Let's say his name was Spider.
Picture a white man's ribs glowing
in the black light behind beaded curtains.
Do I need to tell you the couch cushions were emaciated
as his sunken chest? That his left arm hung on air
like a broken antenna in search of a buzz?
Maybe you already know the reek
of carpet pad marinated by a bong,
and can crawl your way across a floor mined with ashtrays,
bodies and bras. I don't have to remind you
that Spider's the only name she'll need to know,
that skin works the same as cash, and every line is cut
with something she likes to call clean.
I don't have to remind her to pay up front —
to pray he can get it hard, then pray he keeps it soft.
She's already been branded.
It's the smell of semen and Wild Turkey,
lingering in her hair, it's another woman's eyelids
fluttering open, watching from across the room.
It's the way she'll see her every time
a man grips your hips from behind — maybe
she's found the answer to loneliness,
the way to people her world with ghosts.
Maybe she already knew she came here to get fucked
up. That she'll forget the days
but remember it all.

Glitches

Janie's face is a silhouette, backlit against the window.
A chill-sopped sky licks the panes.

In the distance, tree limbs, a gabled roof
are charcoal and shadow.

We meet online, where her leg can shudder
just below the screen, where internet glitches

help me see her for what she was
just a few seconds before. She says it's the parallax

she's chasing, the rawness from rubbing
words against her throat

then waiting for the signal to freeze, the video to lurch —
syllables collapsing into birdsong

that we translate together. *Tell me about your w-
eeeek eeeek eeeek eeeek eeeek*

In the feedback from her speakers,
my voice is an oriole. She shifts in her chair, nods

as if chirps and trills are a language
native to her ears. Our conversation is a call and response.

The hour passes, and behind her the sky grows dim.
I hear the shriek of a chickadee —

see her lips move. Inside the shadows,
the rough bark of the boughs is softly taking shape.

It Was Everyone. It Was No One.

Not my cousin —
both his legs were in a cast.
And not my mom. And not her mom.
And that left everyone else.

I take credit for waking up,
blood and serum dried like shelf mushrooms
along the length of my lips. I take credit for howling
as mom blotted with a warm washcloth,
pried me apart in the tub.

Who did this?   I just woke up this way.
Who did this?   I went to bed alone.
Who did this?   What?

Why can't you remember?
What do you mean no one was with you?

Mom fingered my scalp as if searching for an exit wound
where my memories fled. *Then the truth is,*
you did this to yourself.

I dried off. I got dressed. I smiled
and hugged my cousin, whose legs were in a cast.
And my mom. And her mom. And all my other loved ones.

It was the day after
Thanksgiving and eight people were waking up
at our house.

Missing Pages

I slide the razor blade
along the hump of its spine. Two leaves

unhinge from body and thread
amongst my fingers, as if in sudden freedom

they seek to be rebound. With the cover clam-shelled,
no one can see what's been taken.

From the side, the loss of two sheets is invisible,
because looking broadside at the truth

is a different thing than perceiving it.
I shelve the book, wait for the day

its pages will fall open across your palms —
its binding eager to share the secret

wound. You'll read about
about a floodswept woman, a torrent washing her

out to sea. How her fingers locked onto a tree,
an ocean away from shore.

Collected Evidence

Exhibit A

Fourth grade vocabulary test prompt:
Use the word *fool* in two complete sentences.

She looks like a fool when she wears that hat.
I hope that fool falls down the stairs.

Class, what does it say about the person
who uses the word *fool* as an insult rather than a joke?

I'm returning your tests face down.
One among you needs to reflect. You know who you are.

Exhibit B

In religion class I told the teacher how dad shouts
my first *and* last name when he's angry,

that's how I know Jesus's last name is Christ
and God's last name is Damnit.

I asked her why Jesus had a different name from his dad
and if Mary and Joseph are also Christs.

Exhibit C

I once glanced at the *laundry facility* sign on the door by the gym
and thought it read *Lucifer.*

Routinely saw images of Satan materialize
on bumpy popcorn ceilings and the woodgrain on paneled walls.

Exhibit D

In the rectory Father handed chocolates to the little boys, passed me by without a second look.

Daughter

A midwest man furrows the earth,
lives on the yield of his seeds & struts
in flannel plumage — red as any warning.
Mother said women are made to fit men. She meant
we were formed through impression.
Horseshoes curving from hammer & heat.
always against the anvil. She meant
we were a sacrifice. To my father
daughters that marry well were a point of pride.
I can still hear him smack our mare's rump.
prime fillies come from prime studs. He meant
I was born symmetrical to a man.
Find a strong husband,
& your sons will be good workers. He meant
I needed someone to counteract my frailty.
(wo)man was a prefix— only meaningful when paired.

By Choice

Childlessness has not erased motherhood from my body —
rubbed the archetype clean.

Wide hips advertise lodging. My narrow waist is a neon sign
flickering *vacancy*. I've reached the age

where realtors ask about my children
changing school districts, then shake their heads and mention

friends with infertility. Childlessness
is not a synonym for barren, but it brands me as broken

because I seek no remedy. Because seeking a remedy
implies a fracture that does not exist.

I trace my finger down my breastbone,
translate the ways my chest has cracked. Tumbling

as the horizon bilges me end over end into night.
I pry my ribs apart like wings —

mothering an exit, nurturing a wound. I catch the wind
to birth my voice, thread the names of the moon between my
 teeth:

Milk-Sopped Palm. Eucharist Sky. My belly
is an empty womb. My belly is filled

with my falling.

Body Language

I am laying down
new grammar. Knees, hips,
shoulders — an ellipsis. My body,
a comma in bed that cannot pause. Silent breaths
grind my rhythm into the sheets.

You watch me sleep
through the sound of ice shifting in a glass,
your fork severing waffles on a plate. The laptop
flickers blue — spins the soundtrack
for my dreams. Some nights

I fall asleep alone
wake with my spine in italics, screaming
if you whisper, if you try to tiptoe past. I want to change
the sheets, strip them back and show you
my body

can never walk away
from bed. Even as I rise, I am forever an outline
yellowing on the mattress —
a carbon copy
in sweat.

Drapes

Leave them parted, like lips
gliding on glass

& I'll wake softspun & damp
peeling sheets from my stomach. In the light
glaring off my sweat, we'll watch
a skinwater sunrise

as morning's shaft
daydrifts across my body.
I will roll, blotting belly on cotton,
before I rise.

Puddles will dry into puddles
of salt.

Body Cartography

I know body in terms of permission,
every part sounding like my mother's voice
yes-ing / *no*-ing. She had a judgement
for every sort of flesh. A gridmap
anchored by place. My mother was first
to survey and break my skin
into zones. My whole body
became a cartography of borders.
I've lost my way on this map
where every town shares two names.
No label for the gully where collarbone
blends with shoulder. Her schematics
ignore how touching my neck
is felt in my thighs. When I asked her
about my lips, she had no lessons
for the body's homonyms.
Both of them yes? Both of them no?
I just know that I hear her voice chanting
when my body is hungry,
grinding its way through the night.

Passing Zone

After fourteen miles trekking in the woods,
canopy peels apart and blue sky gleams above the open wound.
It's here the trail joins with a road to cross a bridge.
I walk along the edge. Where jersey wall slopes to asphalt,
dandelions poke up from last year's salt, road dust & crumbling
   leaves.
Below, a scenic byway bisects the park.

I drag my fingers along the thigh high rail.

It would be easy to swing a leg over the barrier,
to lean a bit too far. I stare down at the double yellow lines.
A car passes under as it barrels north. The hikers ahead of me
   hug the shoulder
and disappear back into the woods, safe on the other side.
At my feet the dandelions are a dashed yellow line
running the entire span.

Deadfall

I have yet to spot them.
Branches rubbing together, creaking
in the breeze. Somewhere in the tangle, limbs have crossed
and the bark falls as powder to earth. I rest
on unleavened ground, where grass has yet to rise
to the occasion. On the forest floor, only weeds
have the courage to poke up
where I lay down.

I was never any good at trust,
the game of falling backwards into someone's arms,
except once, sweating and sticky from the broken milkweed.
That day it didn't matter if they had my back. My heels
were already tilting, my arms — false wings.
A suddenness of clouds as the tree line
tugged the sky before my eyes.

A gamble is the form of faith
I practice. Laying with outstretched limbs
groaning in the canopy above — my body adjacent to prayer.
Boughs sweep the sky into my view,
sweep it out again.

Facing Myself

After a scalding shower,
blushing skin camouflages rosy scars.
I am washed—
Naked,

with a cataract of steam,
blunting my sight. Feathering
jagged edges.

The mirror opposite the curtain—
inescapable.

I will myself to look.

Press my finger to the foggy glass,
its flesh spreading like thighs on a metal chair.
I recoil—

A pupil of vibrant colors
pierces the haze where my finger touched.

Expanding like an iris in dim light
when I lean close.
Constricting

as I pull away,
palms gripping the sink rim.
Searching for the perfect aperture

to erase my seams, spotlight smooth skin.
Tuck tender parts
into the fog.

I'm still learning to see—

Occasionally running for cover,
blurring the pupil with my hot breath
when I've had enough.

I Ask Forgiveness

for the way I whispered
fuck you instead of *amen.*
and for the way I wanted to, but never did,
say it loud enough for anyone to hear.

because every mole must hide
because some moles lose their nails digging
and others surface clean fingered
but choking.

for thinking god fucked his son
with a childhood. and jesus fucked us all
with his example. and nobody fucked poor mary
except they did.

because every daughter is an echo
and every echo is a sound borrowed from its maker.

here, a nativity in stained glass
is backlit by a votive, is committing sins
of omission.

i go on wanting
its colors to show manure below the crib. blood,
red as cherries, stippling the straw.

here is a nativity that tells a story of god as a brood parasite
like the cowbird & the cuckoo
and joseph as a tool.

i put coins in the box. put a match to the wick.
because every mole must be
smoked out.

dropping to my knees is the way
my own body echoes.

yesterday i counted
all the way to seven with my finger in the flame.
this blister is the shape of penance.

one…two…three…
the skin won't burn until its water is boiled away.

Reflections

A man in a leather vest
tugs a towel from his beltloop,
dries the glass before he pours.
He makes no show, just palms
a crumpled twenty & tucks it in the till.
He understands that dimness is required
for colors to shine. A neon Rolling Rock sign
drool down the wall—its light no less
subject to gravity. We slump,
with elbows on the bar, and lint in our drinks.
Clockwise. Counterclockwise.
Stirring a cocktail. Peering into a well.
Moving the ice cubes will never reconfigure
my reflection. Floating atop bourbon,
eyes shimmer in a hammock of bone.
Amber. Unblinking. Regardless
which way the tumbler swirls.

Grace

hunger spills like bare light —
too thin to cup between our hands.
one palm, two palms

opening up the darkness. we know
where to make our hinges,
how to fold our thirst

along its seam. across hickory
boards laid down without leaves
we reach for nuts, the last of the apples

and bowls to fill. with rain
slicking the windows like braided rivers,
we lace our fingers,

bow our heads
in prayer. our knuckles are locked together,
tightening as only fists might do.

Boundaries

Waist high in ironweed,
   fly after fly lands on the blooms

of blood. Flesh is smoother below the scabs
   I scratched away. So many layers of skin

hold body to bone, that we are forced to live
   adjacent to suppression. Every journey is a search

for rupture. That first swelling
   within a womb, wrangling with the cord and mother

pushing us out into the air, is the initial act
   of separation. If wholeness is to perforation

as communion is to puncture,
   then every connection brings its own pain.

So I made my own entrances.
   Do you remember forceps pinching skin

above my navel? The wide gauge needle breaking
   trail for the ring? Then jab after jab —

a butterfly translated into pinpricks.
   None of it made me permeable. I lie

in the ironweed, adding breath after breath to the breeze.
   It's only after I've closed my eyes,

that I hear the cicadas' song inside of me —
   a tinnitus welling within my head.

Heavy Metal

Long hair was bound to his forehead
by a flannel's amputated arm. Its plaid print

sucked away sweat before it dropped
to the shoulder. On state road 121

Firebirds and Chargers revved,
peeled off in twos. Most Saturday nights

he parked below the billboard's halo of moths
leaned back against the driver's side door,

and flicked his Zippo. Warrant and Poison poured
so loud from his open windows that crushed cans

hit the pavement in silence. He blasted 8-tracks
smoked pot and joined the union.

After a year of jackhammers and angle grinders,
his Plymouth turned over without a roar

but he learned to hear it through his grip on the steering wheel,
the gear shift vibrating on the floor.

He sank his paychecks into subwoofers and bass
and his chest began to pulse

with Iron Maiden. But it was iron*work*
that finished the job. He was straddling an I-beam

when molten slag ricocheted behind his welding helmet
burned its way down a waterless canal.

What sound did he hear as the drum incinerated —
the beat softened by heavy metal?

Taxidermy

There was too much to hold. Too many things
that could not be reduced to skins,

and tacked neatly to the kitchen wall. Shelves
can stand in for a question

when the spoken words would burn like napalm
through even the wettest tongues.

An empty hutch left space for suggestion, it was her way
of asking if she could hold a bit more for him.

It slowly filled with gifts from her son. Uncle Arnie
had returned from war,

but only in name. He reintroduced himself to us
through killing. He healed himself

with the beauty he wrestled from decay. A monarch's wings
pinned beneath a cloche, now rested

on the third shelf. Scarabs and assassin bugs were preserved
in blocks of resin. At the very top,

an opossum stood like a finial,
its hairless tail coiled, canines jutting from open jaws —

forever on the verge of snapping.

Muscle Memory

Grandma lifts the arm with a single finger,
sets the needle down

on the exact groove where silence
sputters and pops,

turns itself around,
as if a circle is just a corner with no end.

She closes her eyes
and loops across the floor, threading

between the chairs
as a tongue knows cartography of tooth-

slick lobes, as a tongue once sliced
orbits round and round

the molar with its chip,
as if safety is parallel to the jagged edge.

Refuge

In the quiet house,
candies have no wrappers. Horehound barrels

are mounded in a glass dish.
She plucks them with a thumb and forefinger

always from the top, so the others do not tumble —
so there is no sound.

In the quiet house, the cuckoo perches atop the clock face —
melodies swollen inside its throat.

Time has not moved forward in years,
which is a recipe for youth, but a sign of aging.

Instead, she keeps beat, waltzing
over moonlit floors. She is moth-flight and cotton nightie.

In the quiet house,
things are just as they have always been.

Acrylic Garden

The woman who painted it got a divorce in the 1950s,
and consoled herself with bobby socks and a bowling league.

When grandpa saw her at the alley and asked her out,
she hooked him with the line,

I wouldn't have another man, even if his asshole
was lined with diamonds.

She taught all us grandkids how to mix concrete,
apply pesticide and coax nightcrawlers up with a hose.

On windy evenings, she'd put tin cans on corn tassels
and let us call the order as she lowered her cheek to a Remington.

She performed miracles of profane language and entertained us
with R rated movies and trips to Dairy Queen.

In the summer, she skinny dipped,
drank Jack Daniels out of mason jars in the screened in porch,

and turned her feet to leather walking barefoot
up the gravel lane and between the fields.

Her favorite color was brown,
so she never confessed to missing summer when it was gone,

or admitted that she was the one who did it —
but every January, the window by the kitchen table would bloom.

From where she sat, hand painted purple flowers
aligned with where the iris beds lay, long dormant under the snow.

Cherry Pie

No one speaks.

We stand by the picnic table
with a hose threading through our feet.

Us cousins empty our pails into a pile,
use our hands to corral the fruit before it rolls off the edge.
Grandma tells us girls

that cherries with holes are not worth keeping,
and the rest need to be rinsed clean.

She points the nozzle at each of us in turn,
then fills a metal pail with water.

There won't be many that float,
but a few will always rise up against a wash.

Those should be cast aside too.

Grandma clamps a cast iron cherry pitter to the table.
She scoops the firmest, most unblemished fruit
into the hopper.

I crank the handle that turns the blades.
Pits slide down a chute. The split flesh splatters
into a bowl.

Anointing

Grandma picked up a handful of the cast-off cherries
and walked away.

We followed her into the shed
where she dropped them into a Mason jar.

Every day we came back to look
at unchanged fruits. Until the fifth day,

when she sat the jar on a scrap of dark leather.
Buttery maggots undulated against the backdrop of the hide.

Grandma pulled back some burlap,
showed us the others she'd left to soak in a cauldron of oil.

Worms wove a lattice across the surface.
Oil suffocated most, and prevented any live floaters from
climbing to the rim.

Grandma hummed a tune as she ladled.
Hummed a tune

as she dipped her finger into the brew,
anointed us on our brows.

Thresholds

   the best entrances   exit
   onto untangled sky
             titanium glare
   of queen anne's lace
          pouring
    the meadow's edge
   over the horizon

   her eyes   were that kind
   of opening
    lids pushing margins
    away
   wild irises   constricting sun
    to a pinpoint

   even then   her world
   was shrinking

   that final summer   she spent
   under the arbor   coaxing
    chickadees
      with peanuts
       in an open palm
    close enough
   where she could still see

through wisteria
coiled above   her narrow aperture
  of sky
       was purple & green
  her sky
was a fading bruise

Tic-Tac-Toe

The buttons on the bedspread
are not sewn in place. I've laid them out,
echoing our last game.

She chose Kelly green,
and I took brass.

Hers pooled at her fingertips,
where the blanket sloped over her thigh.
I kept mine loose, rattling
in my palm.

Every morning the window muntins filleted the sun,
spread its grid across her lap
and we would play.

I still come here to sip coffee, watch light slide
across the empty bed.

For a few minutes, each button gleams
in a square patch of sun.

Inheritance

She handed me her heart,
a red ceramic music box
she painted for me, kiln fired
in the heat of summer, in the dark
of basement, with tiny brushes,
shimmer chalk & glaze. Mamma —
with her hair ragged back by gingham. Hands
knotted, tucking curls under cotton. Hands hinging
the lid & notes hammering. Mamma —
held out a heart that was hungry
as an empty cup, frigid as porcelain
beneath my palms those nights I stayed up
gripping the rim & waiting for the moon
to pass right through. My mamma
is a sunset at dawn, will be an artist waking
to breath's echo in the sink.
This heart is a dam. The melody is a dam.
Her daughter is a damn opening.
She tells me the notes will play
a thousand times before the battery dies & she will live
for as long as I can make it last. Mamma —
molds mortality out of clay, leaves me
with a heart that defines the future
in terms of ration, in terms of choosing which days
are worthy of a play. Tomorrow is now
lifting the lid & listening for the time
when silence will answer back.
Her heart is a fragile thief
I immediately break.

What We Save

I've kept it since we were kids,
a brown bag, crumpled and smoothed
so many times it feels like fabric.
Inside is a bird I've let go to bones,
a button, and an industrial spool for thread —
a wooden bobbin we fished
from the factory floor.

It was the only solid thing
among shards of glass. I remember
your voice saying *antique* as you crouched down,
slid it into the pocket of your coat.
Every sound echoed, as if what happened a second before
was fighting to stay alive — as if this abandoned sweatshop
was still in the business of manufacturing
history.

We shuffled past rows
of sewing machines rusting in shafts of light,
below barn swallows nesting in the rafters.
We did not speak the name of the building
with its windows laying on the ground,
or acknowledge what we were doing
as we kicked up dust, moving from room to room
in bluing light.

Even as I stopped,
scooped up the bird & tucked an indigo feather
into my hair. I could still hear our footsteps —
ghosts trailing just behind.

Mother's Letter

Pressed flat below the book, the letter's crease lines
show how truth can be bent to fit the shape of an envelope.

I tilt the paper into the scissor's blades, separating
the beryl pond from the bullfrog's anthem

on the other side of the shears. The nighthawk swoops again,
gliding through mother's hand. I slice away

the places it hasn't flown—the hayloft,
wisteria vines tangling the arbor gate, which have always been

more of a snare than an invitation. Mother never wrote
of its mournful song, how its wings slice sunset till it bleeds.

I cut around the cobalt sky, leaving room for the nighthawk above
the summer's crown of hickory and oak. I trim

her letter to the shape of a bird. In the window light,
the paper is tissue, her letters—veins

tracing through its wings. The tangle of ink more like a snare
than an invitation.

Haunted

I don't remember where the rag came from originally,
but my mother kept it in a stoneware crock.

Soft as cobwebs, its cotton compresses in my fist
while I dab its corner in lemon oil.

The gun cabinet has glass doors curving around a cherry frame
that I polish with tiny circles.

Her shotgun and rifle butts sit in a row,
their barrels wedged between divots in the wood.

I lean to the side, level my eyes on the work.
My reflection hovers like a ghost across a Remington.

For a second, I see her face staring back at me,
her translucent fingertips brushing along the trigger.

Atonement

We were on the water the first time
I formed a loop and cut it through with my knife.

Blue and white plastic, suddenly unspun,
pulled apart like split skin

in the wake of a blade across the belly. He showed me how to cope
with a frayed end. With the flick of a Zippo

singed strands of nylon drooped before he crushed them
together between his thumb and finger.

Offshore again and neon rope dangling from my fist cuts
the grey haze, coils against the hull.

Its suppleness betrays
the tension required for strength. He sits on the bow

one foot sprawled on the railing, another curled behind.
His movements are practiced. Fishing

inside his breast pocket. Tapping the cellophane end
until a Marlboro shimmies out.

There is the pucker. A calloused hand concealing
an open flame, and then the draw.

Without even looking, he passes the lighter over his shoulder,
pulls the cigarette away from his lips.

I think of the first day he handed me the club,
silver eyes open the whole time

as I swung it down. Scales splattered my bibs
while he looked on, taking drag after drag.

Today, he's cut the engines while I tie off buoys,
set pots before slack tide. Today,

my fingers will burn.

To My Brother Who Hardened

You were mollusk soft
before the brine dried into your shell, before dad
used us for his sport. Brother,
I can still see us.

Chin deep
beyond the breakers,
with our toes anchored beneath the rocks,
standing upright on the ocean floor.

Fish circled our legs
nibbling the sunscreen from our skin.
To dad, we were living chum, our heads
marking the school below.

You said we were unpaid mercenaries,
ushering death toward this shoal for his amusement.
You realized that day, what it meant
to be predatory.

Dad cast from shore,
reeling his lure past us into evening,
snaring sheepshead and snook. Our guilt
kept us from watching the massacre.

Instead, we faced the open sea,
where sand scurried from the darkening depth—
dried into land. I imagined
its escape.

Once, you grabbed my shoulder
as a dark shadow swam between us.
I saw your pupils high-tiding, submerging
the ring of blue.

Your eyes became the ocean.
Aqua, then turquois, then navy, then
blackness—the heaviest light,
reflecting nothing back.

Say My Name

Before I could reach the cupboard without a stool,
but after I was big enough to pour the jug,

is when it slipped —
the plastic cup kids use so they don't break

when dropped. Not every design meant to avoid disaster
plays the part.

The last time dad spoke my name, it spilled out
with the grape juice.

When he said I could earn my name back
only after the shag

no longer bore a purple stain,
he meant a kid is worthless until the bruises heal —

that the wounded are the ones who do the wounding.
After the crop tops and low-rise jeans

but before I learned to handle my bourbon
at parties, I'd hear my name

as an unearned gift. Every man who spoke it had come
to collect their debt.

Blame

A loose loop of wire
rings the bottom of the fence.
Juts into the footpath between fields
like slipknot looking to snare.
Can't call it a mistake —
you never make any of those. Let's say
this fence post and its crossmember
is the closest thing our farm has to a crucifix.
Christ hung there till he was nothing more than a rail
for his crown of thorns to shimmy
as it dropped to the ground.
Yes! Blame it on Jesus for littering —
that's how the coil of barbed wire got here.
The real blasphemy would be calling it your sloppy repair
because the sky was already spitting, crickets
were already squeaking, and blisters
were already flooding your gloves.
But I have no excuse. For two years,
I've stepped around our lord and savior's sin —
a barbed halo rusting in the grass.
But today, I snag my cuff.
My jeans tear. Eyes tear. On my knees,
face to the weeds. Boots circle heel to toe.
Your jeans are frayed, because coming slowly undone
is the mark of a man, but a sudden rip
just makes me an easy mark. Your kick scuffs
the dirt and seed husks loft into the air.
Tumbling. Tumbling.
The more I blink, the more I see.

Ritual

It wasn't the splinters
plucking fabric in the crook of my arm
that made me hate collecting kindling.
It was becoming Pavlov's dog — the anticipation
of wadding newspapers,
of opening the damper
of combustion.

Fire was our family
attempt to moth ourselves together.
Mom, cross stitching in her own circle of light.
Dad, orbiting with a cigarette, already
glowing red. All of us
passing by the blaze
in intervals

before moving away
as another made their approach.
I would sit on my hands, squeeze my eyes
and count to three. Tap out three with my toe,
and repeat it all again. Seized
by the urge to throw
my teddy bear

into the fire,
to grab the poker and roll a log
across hearth, and onto the carpet. Those nights,
I'd go to bed as the flames died, clenching the blankets
in my fists while people slept —
while embers glowed
in an empty room.

Tire Swing

The balloon, now withered on its string,
is still tied around a vase. Petals have unhinged
and come to rest as a mosaic on the table —
one more thing I'll be guilty of
wiping away.
In our house, amends are no more than a burden.

Dad hangs his apology over a limb,
gives me an eyelet I'm expected to thread —
a tire swing is his answer
to shattered dishes, a wife who is mistaken
for her flesh and a daughter who is only a fraction
of them both.

The porch step is saddle backed
where I sit at sunset, wrapped in the silence I find
outside. I harden myself in the cool air and wait for the voices
to stop, for the screen door to slap. For my father
to walk out, motion me to follow,
then give the tire a nudge.

He needs me to ride it out. On this land
where I learn to shoulder his act of contrition,
forgiveness is a theft. Years of rain have ripened the rope.
I kick off with one leg, listening for it to snap.
The bough only groans, dips like the porch stoop
that expects my weight.

Cut Me a Switch

I always go for birch,
stripping my clothes but not the branch.
I leave it jagged.

   This is my choice.

handing him one that's supple and snappy.
One that cuts as he whips.

   I've never been able to trust

my body to do what's best.
I'll scratch with my fingernails
when the itch comes, when the healing begins.

   Making camo of scars

I am vanishing with every line,
becoming striated as the winter woods.

   Switching and striping.

Switching and striping.
One day I'll stand still amongst the trees
watch him pass right by.

Whitewashed / Washedwhite

in the woods at night
there are no violets i must work to avoid
just a cushion of plants, greyscale underfoot —
silver films of dew reflecting whatever truth
the moonlight holds.   it's the same way a father's fist
tunneling through gypsum, powders itself bloodless —
as if all white knuckles were born
out of fear.   i hoard flour for lean times,
but never have enough courage to open the cupboard door.
each rolled paper lip is an unbroken seal,
a reminder that my palm still retains
its sweaty edge. i do not run my finger under the glue
and dust my knuckles white
out of fear.   *i glue silver films of dew*
to the sweaty edge of the woods at night.
i hoard whatever truth
the moonlight holds. a reminder
i do not run my finger under the rolled paper lip of plants.
i must work   on reflecting the greyscale underfoot.
i dust my palm with a cushion of flour,
as if all white knuckles were born the same way a father's fists
tunnel through gypsum, but never have enough courage to open.
  out of fear,
for lean times, the cupboard door still retains
an unbroken seal.

Because

red hair in the woods is a giveaway in all seasons except autumn,
and you ran for the tree line in July.

because brown corduroy pants don't color you into underbrush,
don't become your coat of bark

because the fabric may rib your legs like a walnut trunk
but you'll never be hard as wood.

because twilight is always shaking inside your eyes, and daybreak
is how your chest splits after night is through.

because you wipe your palms on your thighs but the lint still clings,
leaves a map of your sweat exposed.

because you are wet but have never been mistaken for rain,
you listen to your own patter. running.

because of hands. because shouts. because of that piss in your bed
they're on the verge of wringing you dry.

because you're not colorfast,
your purple skin will always fade to brown.

Dreaming of Time

There is no pendulum
slicing the air. Metal pinecones hang from chains,
measuring time in gravity.

Instead of the cuckoo,
it's a flycatcher's mad swoop,
the wasp, still wriggling in its beak,
swallowed whole. The bird recoils into the clock face
doors swing shut behind,
then silence.

Today, I learned that you are living
in fast forward. You tell me how you've aged into an old man
who will never grow old, how you want to unwind

the hands. I nudge them back
before midnight, stand with my ear to the wood,
listening for a beak to softly peck, for gizzard gears to grind.
The dial hums below my fingertips. I press
my thumb across the doors
and wait.

Can you hear it where you are? Crickets strike the hour
somewhere —

in a separate darkness.

How Time Runs Out

    His clock buffs down,

the thicker minutes. A dial, thin as onion peel

    hangs broadside. We don't see

        its frail edge,

    only a circle —

the shape of hour. There is no hand for depth.

    His body measures minutes

        in volume.

    The belly swells,

where kidneys rest above the bed, below the ribs.

    Layering time into a sphere.

        Nodules,

    like grapes in April,

are a clutch of eggs by October. We wait for the yolks

    to burst — his chest to slacken,

        to sallow.

Distillations

banshee,
   you must have studied us.

years ago, making salt from the sea,
   boiling water away

till crystals remained. we were chasing
   something undiluted. now everything

is a reduction. my father is evaporating
   away from his bones.

distillation is what happens
   during illness. i watch his life

condensing inside a room. skin
   shrink wrapping his body. i'm waiting

for you, banshee. hopes raising each time
   a fox screams or a kettle squeals.

your *silence* disappoints me,
   but i understand why you wait.

you learned patience at the shore,
   watching us haul jugs from the surf.

we taught you the value of seasoning —
   trading smooth skin for salt.

showed you how every hunger pines for flavor.
   when his wasting is through,

what's left of him will be pungent
   as dried ocean on your tongue.

The Orange

Cigarette smoke
burns my eyes in a memory where there's nothing
but the dim suggestion of pucker lines
like rays around his lips.

In the dining room
a bright square of white is there,
as if we'd already taken down the frame and discovered
the walls had been painted with his breath.

Only we hadn't.

That day I was sitting at the table
as I sectioned an orange. It was my skin that yellowed from the rind —
not the wall. It was a spritz from citrus zest,
not smoke,

that stung me to tears.
The coughing is true. That I didn't like
how his fingers were laced atop the blanket, across his chest
is also true. And I didn't give him the orange.

Only the peel.

I watched him rummage
through ripped pieces gathered in a bowl. Thumbing one edge,
then another. Joining the seams,
his fingers

were finally busy
piecing something back together
that would never hold. I cradled the fruit in my palm,
crushed wedge after wedge between my teeth.

Waiting for His Body

After the call I remember

that kicking a garbage can sounded so hollow
that I bludgeoned it with firewood
that my bare hands felt primal on the timber
that the splinters were a distraction
that I didn't tweeze them—because
that little loss would have been too much

Starting the journey so late

that all the motels were full
that the hours dominoed into dawn
that his face was clinging to his skull
that he died twice one morning
that he survived some more
that the worst version of himself returned

Arriving at truths no one speaks

that my happiness is not soured by his suffering
that his behavior is not the illness
that abuse is his mother tongue
that five years of sobriety gave me a father
that was only a facade
that I will miss the persona more than the man

I will tell you

that I admit to impatience when I'm alone
that I still think about him digging the dog's grave
that he lowered him to the bottom before pulling the trigger
that my ears rang—that relief outweighed anticipation
that delay is a type of denial
that morning he did die

and twice his body did not know.

A Loyal Dog

Wasn't long after
I felt the lumps rising beneath his fur
that he strayed further from the house. Each day
returning a little bit later.

It was four years before I found him
behind sheet metal leaning against an unused stall.
Mandible resting on scattered toes. His spine —
rubble within a leather collar.

Today the air is a blade
parting October down its seam. Family gathers
around my father who cannot leave
his own bed.

I do not come.

Since October 2020

                                                    I haven't

  forgotten it's a bough
that finally pushes the sun below the horizon
or told anyone who might approach,
& inspect the limb for char.   I haven't

  walked slowly enough
by the reservoir in November to recognize
a goose by its waddle or a man
by his gun.   I haven't

  stopped using music
as a dam, turned the dial down & allowed
memories to rush in the wake
of silence.   I haven't

  watched the video of you
I made at the hospital — before the ICU,
before the paddles, the drains,
the delusions.   I haven't

  found a way to give
my tears to you that doesn't cheapen those
I shed for her, or thanked you
for your rage.   I haven't

  cried since before you died
or admitted that your anger is what helped
me dodge my fear of loss,
sidestep grief.   I haven't.

Taking the Dolls Home

Earth is the basin that holds you. A depression
where ashes cling trough to rim, is the body
contoured to its maker.

I will keep the dust from cataracting
the nesting dolls still sloped along your windowsill —
always with their eyes to the land.

Their family is intact, but my thumb finds their seams,
nudges ribs open like hinges. Each figure
is swallowed by its other selves till only one remains.

Obituaries & classifieds glove their enamel
on their journey to a new light,
facing the fields, outside my kitchen window.

I unroll the newspapers.
Smaller dolls shake inside the largest. She is the mother.
Just listen to the rattle — the congestion in her chest.

Landscape

Diaspora

Lifting away, my boot
leaves an hourglass indentation,
tamps the mud closer to the earth's core,
as if supporting my weight
is equal parts strength and give.

Your own boots —
a row of prints alongside mine.
Larger. Sinking deeper on the outside edge.
You break twigs between your fingers,
spit absently to the side,

then shake your head.
You tell me it's the earth rising up against our soles
that makes the prints. It's a family's battle
to plant itself firmly to the ground —
not to be lifted away.

The Final Trip Home

It was fifteen minutes
of fading sun, wisteria and pine —
a quarter hour of lavender pavement
on a stretch with no hills.

It was searching for salt water inside my mouth,
wrapping myself in engine noise
and birdsong. Rolling miles
over red clay.

It's that these roads were skinned and reskinned
since I rode them south two Aprils ago
and the way back home
is not the same.

It's hurricane naked
live oaks dropping limbs,
the dead squirrel on the porch
and twenty feet of stucco crumbling into sand.

It's a silent leviathan —
the blackness behind the door.
The sudden realization that this house is a widow,
an empty nester, somebody's dirty stepchild.

Outside the Window

a buzzard with a missing leg
muscles his way on top of a carcass,
rummaging his head beneath a flap of hide
as other beaks gouge a channel between the ribs.
This is the way

one wound heals another
wounding. Years ago, you told the future,
called my quivering lips *pure sap* as you walked away.
And now bourbon makes sepia of a tumbler,
drowns my reflection

in liquid amber.
It takes time to harden off
in the leading edge of spring. And more time still
to grow soft again, like this deer
whose once stiff belly

is now placental,
and seeping into the ground. You'll never feel the same
earth tucking close around your sides.
Through the glass, ice cubes
bend light around your urn

and I shift my gaze
back to the window, where the one-legged buzzard
is just another mouth ripping flesh from bone.
The race between hunger and healing
is about filling in

the empty spaces.
I can still hear the echo of your .22,
your laughter as the rabbit spasmed and I had to look away.
When it was your turn to shudder and fall,
my grief

packed some final hole.
I waited for a sadness that never arrived,
carried a handkerchief that would never unfold. Even now,
I stare at the injured bird, have no urge
to turn away.

(g)round bones

white sky
blisters January to ground
gouged by ruts. muddy clods
where tires spun
catch the pale glare.
i watch light calcify their shine,
into vertebrae knobbing from earth.
even this spine is lobed.
all things the shape of pregnant.
all bulbs dormant.
along the ditch i collected fossils—
my farm was always
a grave and a nebula.

bleak horizon,
a circle from the widow's watch.
the perfect reflection
for my spinning hem, my looping
thoughts cycling. seasons
falling into winter. we're on a mobius
coiling round
last year's bones littering
fallow fields by the fencerow—
where deer return to earth,
where worms are turning,
w(interring) remains
for birth of spring.

That I May Feel Alive

Mist is silent on my hood.
Only large drops that collect on the tips of trees
make the occasional sound as they drop.

I peel the slicker back,
tilt my naked face toward the sky.
There is no wind to bite across chapped cheeks,
but the skin stings just the same.

I bare my hands,
smooth the icy fog over my forehead and hair.

For years, I've relied on snow and cold rain
to stop me feeling numb.

I am the only animal walking the woods today.

Behind me, my boots have torn the grasses
and the forage lays matted to the mud.

High in the poplar, a squirrel's nest
sags from the damp. Rabbits hunker inside their warrens,
and a vixen rearranges her den.

Their tomorrow always begins with a hunger,
and a hunt.

I am the only animal who is driven out into the weather
by a need to create privation —
to escape

the incandescent glow of home.

Bottomland Bridges

Earth slopes toward it like the shore,
a milk-soft fog

leveling the saddleback land
to the timberline.

Do you remember these lowlands
last winter? How the basin flooded and froze?

I watched you plodding ahead,
following coyote tracks across an ice bridge.

Your coat was red as its kill
when you crouched among the willows

gathering rabbit fur in your mittens
to coat the wind.

Today your aluminum pail
rumbles with walnuts as you meander the hill

to forage a lower clump of trees.
I hear the squeaking handle, the clink of shells

long after your parka fades to pink,
disappears below the haze.

Snapshot

Fog & coal dust
work their alchemy on winter hills,
blotting bark & limbs until the tangle of brown softens
to plum. In a dying town,

even air pollution is an asset —
a curtain that can be closed. At a quarter to seven, a stray dog yelps,
a toddler with a sagging diaper darts
from a trailer,

& Chevy rolls to a stop. It idles
as a child gets out, places a penny on the track.
She lays her ear to the rail. No crossing gate severs the one lane road
ahead of the truck.

Two longs and a short —
the only warning as a Norfok Southern
rounds the bend. Its cyclops headlight pierces the haze. For a
    moment,
grandfather & granddaughter

can see clearly
the bare-chested baby playing in the cold.
After the train passes, the girl bends down to harvest the copper coin,
then heads back to the Chevy.

Arms out, toe to heel
atop the rail, she looks up only after she's sure
the view is blurred by her breath — warm as the penny pressed
into her palm.

Farm as a Silhouette

Naked crowns, black on winter sky,
are studded by crows. The same ones as had been in the field
picking clean the heifer we dozed into a ditch.
Now silent. Now still. Somehow blacker in slack light.
Somehow larger at this distance.

Sun cuts a low cesarean arc.
In twilight, only the canopy remains distinct.
Tree trunks smudge together like charcoal under the thumb.
Birds silhouette high in the branches,
above the rising flood of night.

My grandfather likes to say
this land is the same as when he was a kid.
By this he means the boundaries haven't changed
but everything within them has. By this he means some men
only value what they find along the edges.

Or maybe truth rises at sunset
when the row of stumps is swallowed in shadow,
and treetops behind them transform into the chestnuts that stood
   in his youth.
Even the crows' glinting eyes lose their coordinates.
Only outlines remain.

Better with Time

I watch our barn go grey,
camouflaging itself with the sky.
Storms now pass it over, mistaking it for kin.
It's my reminder that ingenuity comes with aging.

Over time, its hardware crumbled.
Loose sheet metal warbles from the roof when the breeze
lips it just right. I let it flap. Screwing it down
would silence its music.

A crosscut saw hangs above the door
rusting toward the ground. Each raindrop is a new wound.
I sacrifice it in the elements — allow its mural
to reach its conclusion.

Dutch elm took the tree by the silo.
I know it attracts termites, that its branches will snap —
but I let it stand. Every summer, woodpeckers
fledge from its core.

Carrying On

      starling-sewn clouds | cinch tight
over high ground | where women and birds
once gathered | by food & fire

      all that remains | are arrowheads
piercing plough-turned soil | a grinding stone
clutched in the roots | of a toppled tree

      i walk | amidst the rubble
with an apron of bread | to cast into the grass
threaded popcorn | to drape on ironweed

      the flock | forages in a froth
of wing-tossed dew | where ravens once scavenged
scattered bones | by a flint's edge

      birds do not fear | the scarecrow
skewered on his own pike | his shadow a crucifix
falling across | stolen land

No Getting Away

Just this once
I told myself to watch,
stood with my shoulder leaning on the wooden post
holding up the roof of the porch.

Out by the shed
he shoved a metal rod through the doe's Achilles
and hoisted her hand over hand
to hang from the elm.

She peeled,
easy as a thumb-poked orange —
white webs pulling at purple flesh as her hide
shimmied down

past her vacant eyes, to brush at the tips of grass.
Her back legs were splayed,
chained to the bough.
A thick stick

wedged between the ribs
held her open as she steamed into autumn air.
Reaching inside her chest,
he stripped her

tenderloins along the spine,
held each one between the blade and his thumb
before he laid them glistening
on paper.

I crept inside,
turned my back to the door.
Even sunlight cast through the transom onto the foyer floor,
looked like sinew marbled by leaded veins.

Harvest

As if bullets trained me
to be calm — to unquake my breath
and squeeze my finger like a smooth running river.
As if the weeds at the side of the tractor barn didn't grow
through the casings where I stood last year and the years before.
As if the temperature weren't going down
and the price of feed going up.

As if winter didn't demand sacrifice
and November wasn't a threshold for us all. As if I hadn't told you
the echo of early morning rifle fire in the hills was a lullaby
and the steer had just laid down across our table.
If you hadn't named him, hadn't taught him
to take food from your hand, then every meal
wouldn't be made of family.

As if betrayal is an act
of love and love must always lead
to the violence that fills our mouths around the table.
If harvest is the act of choosing family over food,
then family is what makes us pick up the gun,
coax him with a handful of grain. As if trust is a commodity
you raised for me to spend.

At the Table

        morel mushrooms   plucked from the woods,
fried in oil we last used for fish   every morsel becoming
a memory of water.   so much time spent hunched
at the stove   we lied about their taste.
      the punishment of eating them   was penance
for their harvest.   hauling them from the forest
in a plastic sack instead of mesh   not allowing spores to
  fall through
reseed the ground   as we walked. we found answers
      to our sins   a meal without heat
a meal without salt   with only beads of sweat
to brine parsnips into stew.   a table with just enough
game to make us grateful of beef   once more. a drake
  plummets
      into the jaws of a dog.   we pluck
feathers and birdshot   lop off its head with a blade.
duck is a ghost we chew slowly   our molars splitting
breast and thigh   tongues flapping
     like a translation of wings.

Night Vision

Slinging one leg over the sill, I stumble
the gravel lane —

a silver ribbon, where the full moon
wraps itself along the earth.

His car is waiting behind the birch,
too far for the crunch of tires to hitch home on the wind.

We drive to Whitewater Gorge Park,
stow the Chevy behind the auction house down the road

then finish the way on foot. The air is amphibious,
our skin slickens in knee high weeds.

We do not carry flashlights. There are no visitors allowed
at night. There are no visitors

to stand in our way as we lay down on the suspension bridge,
a heaving footpath across the river.

Barely wide enough to lay side by side,
we search for Draco and Libra, listen to boulder-combed

water flowing between the deeper pools below.
Pike gaze up, where the surface is still.

Across the planks of the bridge, our flesh is no more
than a starless patch of their sky

and the gaps between stars are no more than our eyes'
failure to see what's really there.

We didn't hop the gate after dark
because the rules didn't apply.

We snuck in out of fear of being seen
during daylight. Not by others, but by ourselves.

Catching Crawdads

Knee deep in the Whitewater
we squat in the current, lifting stone after stone.

A catfish darts between my legs while striders skate
in a stagnant pool. My nylon shorts balloon

as we sit with our backs to a boulder and the net
resting across your knees.

You tell me again how crawdads can snap twigs
in their claw, how you can hold them

so you won't get pinched. The mason jar is empty
but for water & you

return to rummaging beneath the rocks, swishing
with your net. I trail behind

asking about the snapping turtle
who still held the stick between its jaws

even after you laid it out on the sycamore stump,
even after you brought the hatchet down.

Milk Teeth

Grasshoppers are a heat wave
blurring sky

above the meadow we stirred
with our bare legs.

She stops to finger the sun
peeled skin,

across her lips, two thumbs
dimpling. Her smile

shows me how much farther
split flesh stretches.

We learn to part
thistles with our tongues, swig air

from an empty bottle,
just to feel how transparent things

can be so hard. To swallow,
she squeezes milk

from her teeth.
Our gums were once enameled

with the nipples that we bury one by one
in a matchbox —

a grave we reopen
with each new loss. Our thirst

grows, both of us
asking how we'll drink

long after we've wriggled loose
the final one.

Plum

More of a slippage than a hiss —
like one wet leaf cleaving from another.
                    Strip. After. Strip.
          Skinning a plum with your teeth
is to be equally resigned to sound
and patience.   The peel
is an endless turning.
             Remnant warmth,
where it rested in your palm is the only landmark.
The bruise is a palimpsest of your thumb
      pressing.   Its softness
rises up around your teeth.   Snapping
as its membrane breaks —
more of a felt thing than a noise.   Inside
the puncture, juice wells. This is how the body gives in
to violence.   Strip. After. Strip.
     Raw flesh conjures
a color we cannot name. Dwindling Fire. Predawn Glow.
Kaleidoscope Turning.
                    Bite. After. Bite.

Charcoal on Water

In morning light,
the ice glaring red atop the cinder pit

is a memory of last night's flames —
of embers that rose like lanterns on the updraft
and drifted deeper
in the dark. We held hands

above the flames, burned-in the memory
of winter heat. In June

we chased sparks
tumbling through night air.
We caught the cold light of fireflies between our palms,
and found summer harbored no warmth.

Last night's hiss
was the sound of liquid dying on a bed

of wood and coals.
When you tipped the bucket, water rose to the stars
and froze across the ground. Locking
ash and splinters

inside the puddle — a charcoal
sketch on the surface, a twig reaching toward sky.

Homecoming

It began with snowmelt on the floorboards.
Damp soles freezing to the ground

after I crossed the gravel drive and made contact
with smooth pavers. As my foot pulled loose from the boot,

my body lurched forward, and my sweaty sock fused to the stone
with my next step. I paused,

watched a sparrow hopping across the ice.
She cocked her head at me, as if pondering why I'd stopped

in such an exposed place. It's a decision to double back or push forward,
each step stripping leather, then wool, then skin.

It's that single moment after hot breath wets a hollow fist,
when I must choose between fingers and toes.

My stocking slipped away as I moved on toward the porch.
Standing barefoot on ice, I dared not lift my foot.

I dared not reach my sodden palm
toward the metal knob.

Pond Water

It was a cappuccino,
dolloped with frog egg foam.
It was partially cloudy then overripe plum.
It wore blossoms in the spring and a feather boa
after the coyote came to call. It was a chaos
of wings and runway. It was shattered by the eider's plunge
and puzzled together with wind. It was a siren song.
It was fog before mist, and star-pocked before dawn.
It was pewter sheen and invitation, motor oil
and irritation. It was swamp gas and bog.
It specialized in sunken keys, flooded waders and defeat.
It was a baptism, turned whole-body kiss. It was a curtain shutting
across the muck. It was the stink that never came clean —
the pond that visited our Maytag and never moved out.
It was cat-tailed and fox-drunk and brimming with the snot from deer.
It was a tongue-stippled turtle tea.
It was a rink for striders but an ocean to a paper boat.
It suffered a scum-capped adolescence
before it grew clear. Its guts were stirred by fish
then turned over with our oars. It was ice and hockey blades
then buried in snow. It was four inches thick
before it grew thin. It was insatiable —
constantly licking the dock. It was a diver's delight
and a bullseye that could never bruise. It was a funhouse mirror
when we couldn't face the truth. It was a warm welcome
for our poles' angle, our ankle's dangle.
It was chalked in pollen on a day without breeze.
It was the ripple of a dragonfly landing on my line.
It was one circle expanding around another —a bluegill's mouth,
whirlpooling just below.

Fight, Flight & Freeze

My lips part
with the sound of leaves
slipping loose from dew.
Autumn strips the shine from my tongue,
billows it on the path ahead. We are walking
through my ghost
together.

I tell you
about snakes the color of forest floor
threading our garden to the earth.
How I screamed. How mother ran,
drove her shovel down—
tongue still flicking
from its severed head.

I dreamed of dad
headless at the table,
ladling soup down his neck—
my hand on his shoulder
bracing against the blackness of the hole.
How I screamed. How mother ran,
peeling sheets from my sweat.

Today the garden is still.
Bitter air has driven snakes into their dens,
and shivers from my core.
Will you lift a maple leaf to the light?
Cast red sun upon my skin
while my body
begs for fire?

Compassion Fatigue

Another ten acres scraped clear. Another
another industrial park rising.

I give my unpicked orchard to the displaced
deer & racoons.

Sanctuary will be the taste of fallen apples
wormed into earth.

This fall, my own mouth hosts only breath —
the smell of teeth & lungs. Hunger

is the language of land & sky. Overhead,
chimney swifts pluck midges

from factory smog. The flock has grown thin
as the leading edge of memory.

For now, I replenish their food
by hatching mosquitos in stagnant water.

I worry that I'll grow tired of buying time
to spend in anticipation of grief.

That I'll decide the fruits & insects
only prolong their starvation.

Years ago, I put a bullet through the opossum
struck by the edge of the driveway.

The agony of bearing witness
outweighed the chance he might have lived.

My fingers would curl again
around a trigger.

Industry has cleaned the sky of color.
One day I'll take up a net

& filter the remaining butterflies from the air.
Their wings —

somewhere between confetti & litter.

On Meeting a Shrike

It stopped me dead at first,
the pupil pushing back green irises
flush at its sides — an opening in the woods

you curated. Hawthorns with white blooms,
honey locust limbs locking barbs
above the path

splintering our hill in mulch —
a softer name for shards, trees needling themselves
back into the earth.

That first summer,
I picked raspberries in long sleeves,
skirted the brambles growing along the sunny edge

and finally took the trail upslope, into deep shade.
My collar snagged as I ducked
under the osage orange.

Heavy with hedge apples,
thorns spired from drooping boughs.
I pushed further beneath the canopy, found a place

where things were still
as a bowl of unpunctured water.
Where the only movement was the butcher bird

feeding from the dead
lizard it impaled on the briers —
its stiff tail, a harpoon piercing the July air.

Felling the Sycamore

These are the final stats.

Ankles blistered and oozing,
from a single brush against the sumac.

The shovel's handle splintering away from the metal.
You told me not to pry. Even then, I leaned
with my body weight — until
I heard the crack.

There were my leather gloves stiffened with dried mud,
and the final strip of wood severed with an axe
after the chain slipped its blade.

Because I forgot the oil. Because I didn't bother
to tighten it down. Because I was running
top heavy,

the wheelbarrow, now tipped on its side, is a reminder
of the things I couldn't carry.

And you, backing away

because the trunk was hollowed by carpenter ants,
and you would never concede that this tree

could be held aloft by a trunk returning to dust.

Percolation

Well water pilfers minerals from the land —
flavors our coffee with calcium and buttered loam.

Every snowfall melting, every apple rotting into the ground,
each body scattered below the tree

is filtered by ninety feet of earth and one ruffled sheet
of tissue paper. The aroma is nutty,

our cups brim between our palms. Warm
with the color of walnut bark scorched by a summer bolt.

As we drink it down, daylight is siphoned below the rim
where it mixes with the coffee. The liquid lightens

to chestnut, then acorn, then taupe.
The interior glaze is crackled and stained —

muddy channels form between flecks of enamel.
We swirl our spoons,

dredge up sediment from generations of brews.
They are all gathered here

as we swallow pebble and tree, switchgrass and sky.
As we drink of fallen fruits and fallen hands.

Acknowledgments

I would like to acknowledge my gratitude to the journals who first published many of the poems in this collection, occasionally in slightly different forms:

After the Pause: "Stay-at-Home-Mom," "Passing Zone," & "Collected Evidence"

Atticus Review: "Ghost", Originally published under the title *Inheritance*

Black Coffee Review: "No Getting Away" & "Cut Me a Switch" & "Ritual"

Book of Matches: A Literary Journal: "Glitches," & "Milk Teeth"

Bracken: "Felling the Sycamore"

Burningword Literary Journal: "Inheritance"

Dodging the Rain: "Because," "The Final Trip Home," "Waiting for His Body," "A Loyal Dog," & "Fight, Flight & Freeze,"

Empty House Press: "I Saw Him Take the Sheets," "Tic-Tac-Toe," & "Windows"

Eunoia Review: "Dreaming of Time," "Grace," "Muscle Memory," "On Meeting a Shrike," "Refuge," & "Taking the Dolls Home"

Feral: A Journal of Poetry and Art: "Conception"

Front Porch Review: "Better with Time," & "Percolation"

Halfway Down the Stairs: "Acrylic Garden"
House Journal: "How Time Runs Out"

The Inflectionist Review: "At the Table," "Compassion Fatigue," "Distillations," & "To My Brother Who Hardened"

Misfit Magazine: "It Was Everyone. It Was No One."

Passengers Journal: "Rust Belt"

Poetry Online: "Harvest"

Prometheus Dreaming: Whitewashed/Washedwhite

River Heron Review: "By Choice"

Rust + Moth: "Deadfall"

Sepia Quarterly: "Taxidermy"

The Shore: "Body Cartography" & "Visual Distortions"

Sky Island Journal: "Plum," "Quarry," "Cherry Pie," "Farm as Silhouette," "Returning to Water," "Say My Name," "Night Vision," "Tire Swing," & "Facing Myself"

SOFTBLOW: "Bottomland Bridges," "Carrying On," "Heavy Metal," "Outside the Window," & "Janie's Elegy (Originally published under the title Flashback)

Trampset: "I Ask Forgiveness"

Turtle Island Quarterly: "Atonement," "Pond Water"

Typishly: "(g)round bones"

Additionally, I would like to thank my friends, family and writing partners who have been an endless source of encouragement. I've tortured Scott, Monica, Danita, Bonnie, Anna, Phillip, Karen, Ezra, Millie, Renee and Lorraine with early drafts of these poems. I'm forever indebted!

About the Author

Lorrie Ness was born in Indiana and currently lives in Virginia with her husband and a menagerie of pets. She completed her doctorate in psychology from the University of Tennessee and her writing is deeply influenced by the complexities of human relationships and our connections to the natural world. When she is not writing, she can be found hiking, photographing insects, and playing in the dirt. Her previous works can be found in a variety of journals.

www.ingramcontent.com/pod-product-compliance
Lightning Source LLC
Chambersburg PA
CBHW061802070526
44586CB00023B/2672